Meet me on
St. Simons Island

Meet me on
St. Simons Island

TIMELESS IMAGES AND FLAVORFUL RECIPES
FROM GEORGIA'S REMARKABLE ISLAND RETREAT

Mary Lawson
Editor

Daisy King
Recipe Editor

Printed in the United States of America

ISBN: 978-0-87197-564-5

Mary Lawson *Editor*
Daisy King *Recipe Editor*
LeAnna Massingille *Cover Designer*

Published by

SOUTHWESTERN
Publishing Group

2451 Atrium Way • Nashville, Tennessee 37214
800-358-0560
www.historichospitalitybooks.com

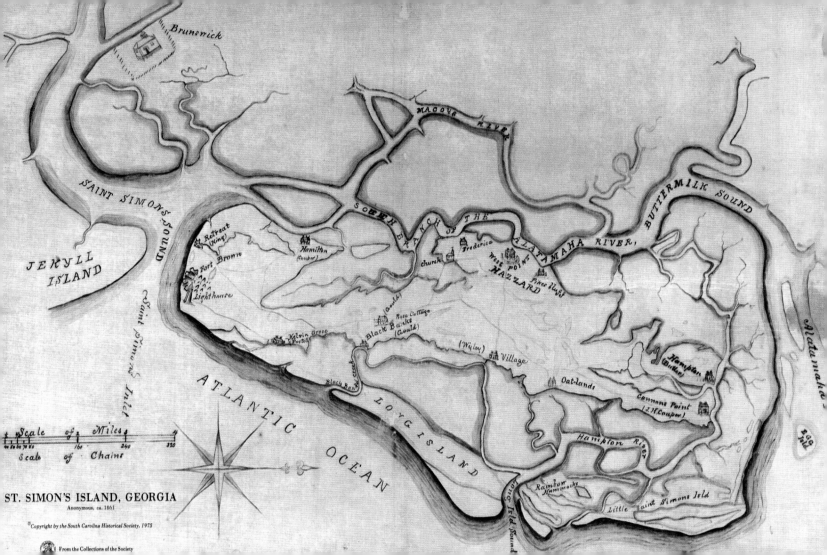

Brunswick

MACOYS RIVER

SAINT SIMONS SOUND

JEKYLL ISLAND

SOUTH BRANCH OF THE ALATAMAHA RIVER,

BUTTERMILK SOUND

Saint Simons Inlet

Retreat (King)

Fort Brown

Lighthouse

Hamilton (Couper)

church

Frederica

West Point

HAZZARD

Pikes Bluff

Alatamaha

(Gould)

Rose Cottage

Black Banks (Gould)

Melvin Grove (Postell)

(Wylay) Village

Hampton (Butler)

ATLANTIC OCEAN

LONG ISLAND

Black Bank Creek

Oat-lands

Cannont Point (J.H.Couper)

Egg Isld

Hampton River

Rainbow Hammocks

Long Isld Sound

Little Saint Simons Isld

Scale of Miles

Scale of Chains

ST. SIMON'S ISLAND, GEORGIA

Anonymous, ca. 1861

Introduction

Dear Reader,

In creating our Historic Hospitality series of books, it is my sincere desire, as publisher, to present beautifully crafted books that relate the cherished history of each property, highlight beautiful historic and contemporary photography, and offer delicious recipes unique to the property to make the perfect memoir of your visit or a very special gift for a friend. We are proud to include historic St. Simons and Sea Island Georgia, as one of our featured Historic Hospitality sites.

It is our pleasure to share its story here with you.

Sincerely,

Roger Conner
Southwestern Publishing Group, Inc.

ST. SIMONS ISLAND

The treasured lighthouse on St. Simons beams its welcome to visitors from around the world and beckons their discovery of its intriguing history and enchanting beauty.

THE STAGE IS SET

Some two thousand years before the time of Christ, St. Simons Island was first inhabited by Native Americans, many of whom were eventually known as the Timucuans and the Guales. By the mid-sixteenth century, Spain had come into her own as the most powerful nation on earth and had thoroughly staked out her claim in the New World to conquer the land for its own purposes. Religious fervor was the motive for the early colonial effort, and primary emphasis was placed on spiritual conversion rather than colonizing for material gain. It was the French who prompted Spain to settle the area on a permanent basis. The Protestants of France were rebelling against the Catholics, and the French queen decided that a colony in the New World could serve as a haven for the persecuted Protestants as well as a base for raiding the treasure fleets of Spain. Spain's roots were entwined with the Catholic faith, and her colonizing and conquering armies were accompanied by men of the cloth. The Jesuits, respected throughout Europe for their piety as well as their scholastic achievement, were selected to convert the Native Americans, who were reluctant, however, to receive the Catholic religion. As the priests made more and more intrusions into their way of life, sporadic and bloody confrontations ensued. The Timucans and the Guales were destined to share a common fate in the final drama that awaited them.

"Landing of the Spanish on The Golden Isles" (1567)

THE DRAMA UNFOLDS

With the arrival of European civilization, the Timucuan and Guale cultures were doomed to extinction. From 1606 to 1655, the Spanish missionary effort reached its zenith as the Franciscan missions reflected a steady growth with seventy missions from Florida north to St. Catherine's Island. By 1617, half the Christian Indians had died of pestilence; some eight thousand were still alive. In 1663, Charles II of England granted to eight Lords Proprietors all the land between Virginia and La Florida. By 1675, only four Guale mission towns remained. The probability of attack from the English and the Indians loyal to them was now a constant fear to the Spanish. The Chichimecos returned in 1680 to attack the towns of Santa Catalina and San Simón. The confusion and helplessness of the missionary and refugee Indians mounted as English pirates terrorized the Mocama and Guale coast in 1683. The following year, San Buenaventura de Guadalquini was ransacked and burned by pirates, and St. Simons Island was abandoned forever by the Timucuans who, for untold centuries, had called it their own. After almost a century and a quarter under the cross and sword of Spain, the Mocama and Guale Indians were no more—their land soon to be known as Georgia.

THE WAY OF WAR

Today's state of Georgia was the center of conflict between Spain and Britain for centuries. When England laid claim in Georgia, the island became a military base two years after General James Oglethorpe founded the colony of Savannah. In 1736, Oglethorpe built Fort Frederica as a permanent English settlement to defend against possible attack by the Spanish from the south. In addition, a military road was built southward as well as a battery named Fort St. Simons as fortifications on Jekyll Island and Cumberland Island to the south. In 1742 a Spanish fleet with three thousand men from St. Augustine indeed attacked St. Simons from the south. Oglethorpe withdrew his men from the battery back to Frederica. The Spanish were led into an ambush in the marsh. So many Spaniards were slain that the battle became known as the Battle of Bloody Marsh. The Spanish withdrew, thinking they had been surrounded by a superior force. After Oglethorpe's return to England in 1745, the troops stationed at Frederica were withdrawn. The town of Frederica reached its high tide in the mid 1700s, but then quickly deteriorated and was eventually destroyed by a fire leaving only echoes of the past. The ruins are still visible today. A few settlers remained on the Island to harvest the ancient live oaks. Cutting of timber made way for the next era to arrive on the stage of St. Simons.

A NEW WAY OF LIVING

The rich delta soil of St. Simons was ideal for agriculture. During the latter part of the seventeen hundreds, several South Carolina planters came to coastal Georgia bringing their slaves with them to clear the land and work the fields. Though many experimental crops were planted, it was special, fine long staple cotton, which became known as Sea Island cotton, that was the staple crop of all the plantations of the coastal area. It brought much higher prices than the short staple variety grown inland, and was used for only the finest cloth and lace. More than a dozen thriving cotton plantations occupied the length and breadth of St. Simons and in order to support the industry, the use of slave labor became a way of life that flourished on the island from 1749 until the Emancipation Proclamation in 1863, even though in 1798, the state legislature prohibited the direct acquisition of slaves from Africa. Rather than eliminating importation, however, it gave rise to the slave smuggling trade along the isolated coastal islands. Sadly, tradition has it that slaves were brought ashore on the banks of the Dunbar Creek at a spot known today as Ebos Landing. The leader of the Ebos, a proud and noble tribe of Nigeria, led his people into the waters of the creek where they drowned themselves rather than submit to slavery.

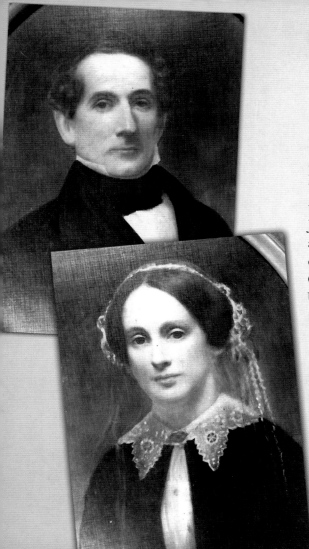

A RICH HERITAGE

There were four plantations in particular that formed the cornerstones of a way of life that endured for three-quarters of a century. Major Pierce Butler, an officer in the British Army, established Hampton which became one of the largest plantations in the South. In 1804, the plantation provided sanctuary for Vice President Aaron Burr, a fugitive from public indignation over the duel in which Alexander Hamilton was killed. Cannon's Point was the home of the John Couper family. John, known for his magnetic personality, had an interest in agricultural experimentation and earned the respect of his peers through his experiments with various seeds of Sea Island cotton that improved its yield. Couper sold the tract on which the St. Simons lighthouse stands today to the United States government for the sum of one dollar. James Hamilton, the long-time business partner of John Couper, built the plantation he named for himself on the land known as Gascoigne Bluff. He traveled to far places of the world and brought seeds of exotic plants to his friend John Couper who was very interested in horticulture. Hamilton's plantation became one of the richest on the island and he became one of the country's first millionaires. Lying adjacent to Hamilton Plantation on the southern tip of the island was a tract originally settled by James Spalding. In 1804, Major William Page, a South Carolinian who had managed the Hampton estate for Pierce Butler bought the old Spalding property and named it Retreat. He proceeded to build it into one of the greatest cotton plantations in the South.

DRASTIC CHANGE

The arrival of the Civil War would mark the end of an era and change island life forever. St. Simons was a strategic location that could supply food for soldiers, serve as a base for raiders and blockade-runners, and command the entrance to Brunswick Harbor. When the Southern coastline was blockaded by the Federal fleet, 1500 Georgia troops manned batteries on the island's coast. Cannon fire was heard on the island in December 1861, and Confederate troops retreated in February 1862, after dynamiting the lighthouse to keep its beacon from aiding Union troops. Soon thereafter, Union troops occupied the island, which was used as a camp for freed slaves. Federal warships soon patrolled the coastal waters, and the U.S. Navy assumed jurisdiction of St. Simons Island. During the latter half of the war, little or no activity occurred on St. Simons. When the war ended, the island would never again prosper as an agricultural community. Upon the planters return, they were greeted by utter desolation. The fields were overgrown, most of their homes were uninhabitable, and ex-slaves claimed the land under eighteen federal land grants. It took several years for the land titles to be restored to the island families. The former way of life was over; however, it was not long before Hamilton Plantation brought a new industry to the island.

Kings Road   "The Retreat"

BUILDING NEW HOPE

Economic conditions began to improve on the island a decade after the Civil War when the first lumber mill was built by A. G. P. Dodge. The island offered an ideal location to process the vast stands of eastern Georgia timber, easily obtained from destitute owners at little cost. Additional mills were built offering every man an opportunity to work regardless of race. The nucleus of the growing community was at St. Simons Mills, as it was known, on Gascoigne Bluff. The sawmill industry flourished on the riverbanks boasting a post office, the company store and offices, telephone and telegraph services, warehouses, commissaries, a school, and St. James Union Church. St. Simons Island was now shipping lumber all over the world, and it was not unusual to see as many as twenty ships from Atlantic and European ports anchored in the Frederica River, guided there by the new lighthouse, rebuilt in 1872. It was at St. Simons that the timbers were sawn for the construction of the Brooklyn Bridge. The feverish activity of St. Simons's lumber industry would end in its demise, for in the early 1900s most of the available timber had been cut and the over-harvesting of timber would number the days for the St. Simons Mills. The Hilton-Dodge Company, as it was now known, ceased to operate on the island in 1906.

CROSSING OVER

Since economic times continued to change on the island, it was fortunate that a wooden pier was already built in 1887 providing regular ferry service to and from the mainland and bringing an ever-increasing stream of summer visitors. In 1888, the Hotel St. Simons, located at the present site of Massengale Park was built and upon arrival on the island, guests were conveyed by mule-drawn trolley from the pier to the rambling hotel in the dunes. Although the original Hotel St. Simons burned in 1898, another structure just as imposing, appropriately named the New Hotel St. Simons, was built on the same site about 1910. As the island's new identity as a seaside resort prospered, the pier became a center of activity around the turn of the century. Two hotels were built at its base flanked by a pavilion, bathhouse, and huge wooden water slide. The mule-drawn trolley was replaced by a small steam-engine tram that in turn gave way to a motorized trolley car. The large grassy field between the pier and the lighthouse was utilized for many years as the summer training camp for the Georgia Militia allowing soldiers to enjoy the island as much as the vacationers. In 1924, a five-mile roadway called the Fernando J. Torras Causeway, was completed and permanently connected the island to the mainland. Wooden bridges spanned the marshes, creeks, and rivers between Brunswick and Gascoigne Bluff and automobiles were soon a way of life on the island.

PAVING THE WAY

The island continued to prosper and in 1928 The Cloister, a world-renowned resort hotel, was opened on Sea Island. Years later in 1941, the King and Prince Hotel opened its doors just in time to be used as a naval officers' billet in World War II. The war came quickly to St. Simons. In the early hours of April 8, 1942, explosions reverberated over the south end as two oil tankers were torpedoed a few miles off the island. Both ships sank and twenty-two crew members were killed. Survivors were rescued and brought for debriefing to the historic Coast Guard station, now one of three remaining stations out of some forty-five of the same design started in 1935 under the WPA program. On the mainland, the U.S. Navy used McKinnon Airport as a home base for torpedo bombers and blimps operating from the new Glynnco Naval Air Station playing an important role in protecting coastal sea routes for much of the conflict. As a result, it was the military that improved the island's roads and airport and built a much-needed sewer system, which gave the island a better infrastructure to support the subsequent development boom of the 1950s and 1960s. The war years had introduced the many charms of St. Simons to thousands of young men from all over the country, and its appeal was no longer a closely-guarded secret.

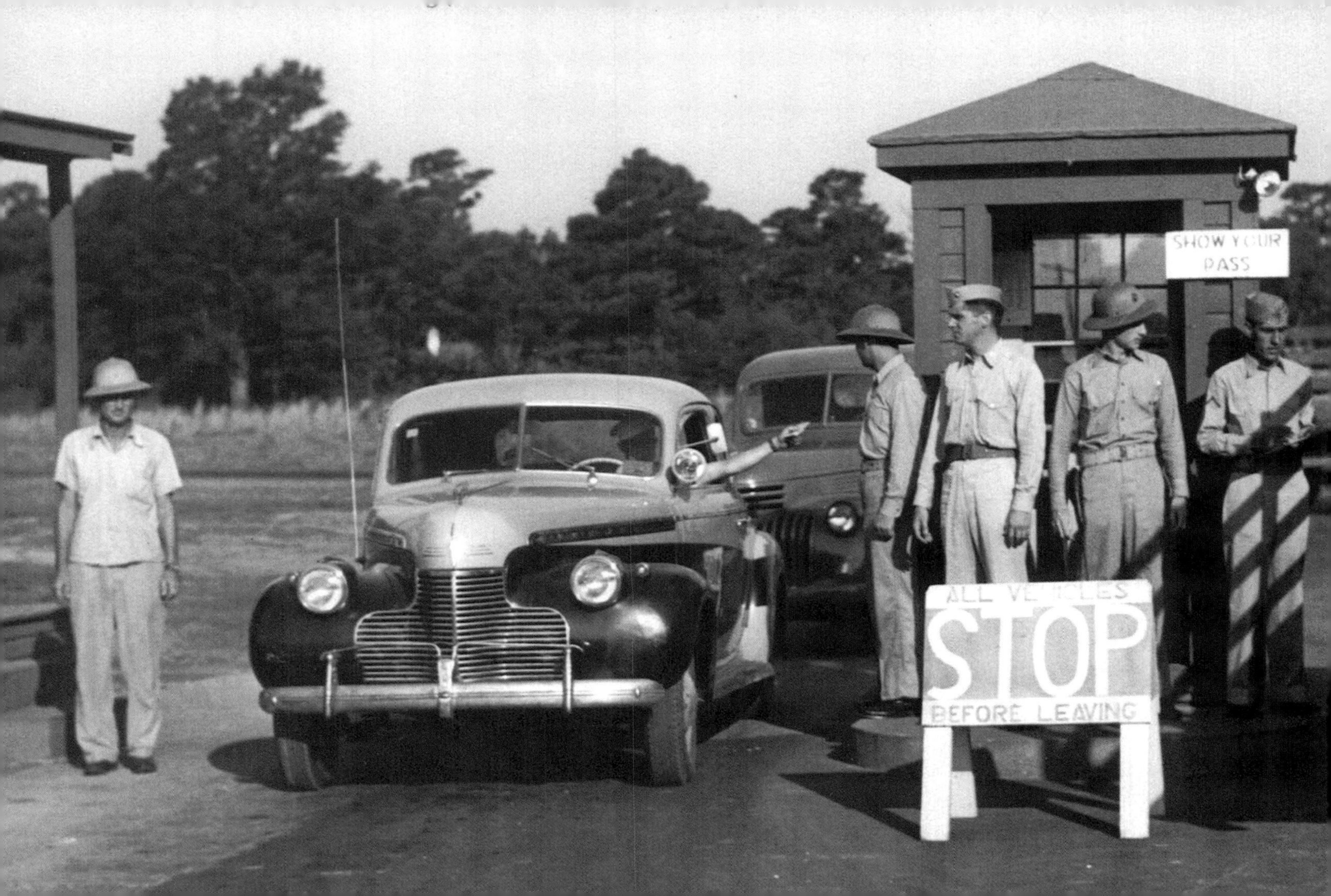
SHOW YOUR
PASS
ALL VEHICLES
STOP
BEFORE LEAVING

A PLACE OF ENCHANTMENT

St. Simons Island, nestled between the lush subtropical barrier islands of Sea Island, Jekyll Island, and Little St. Simons Island just off the Georgia Coast, is the largest of these "Golden Isles" so named because of the golden hue of their vast marshlands. The island still possesses the same enchanting lure as it did hundreds of years ago. It is a place where fascinating history abounds and remarkable beauty surrounds. Visitors are not only confronted with the legacy of its diverse heritage in places like historic Fort Frederica, the hauntingly beautiful Christ Church, the tabby ruins of the antebellum plantations, and its fully operational and tourable lighthouse, but they are delighted with its live oaks dripping in Spanish moss, lovely beaches, coastal wildlife, panoramic marshes, and glowing sunsets. Today, as a tourist resort community, the island still offers golfing, boating, fishing, swimming, bicycling, seaside shopping, and exploring, not to mention the opportunity to sample native cuisine at the local delectable eateries. But more than that, it is an unforgettable experience. Perhaps Georgia poet Sidney Lanier said it best over one hundred years ago when he immortalized the beautiful stretches of marsh in his poem "The Marshes of Glynn."

"Oh, what is abroad in the marsh and the terminal sea?
Somehow my soul seems suddenly free
From the weighing of fate and the sad discussion of sin,
By the length and the breadth and the sweep of the marshes of Glynn."

The Cloister Hotel, Sea Island, Ga.

ONE MAN'S DREAM

Sea Island, a thin Holocene barrier island guarding St. Simons Island to the east, consists of two thousand acres of marsh, dunes, beach, and developed maritime forest. Rising from humble beginnings, it is now considered one of the finest resort and residential communities in the world. Once a fishing ground for Native Americans, the island passed through the hands of several owners before Howard Coffin purchased it in 1926 for $349,485.17. The island was a relatively untouched wilderness when Coffin purchased it, and its transformation into a resort area became his passion. Coffin, founder of the Hudson Motor Company, and his wife Matilda fell in love with the beautiful islands of coastal Georgia and purchased Sapelo Island, just north of Sea Island, for $150,000 in 1911. They also purchased land on the southwestern side of St. Simons Island and formed their new company, Sea Island Investments, Inc., which was later renamed the Sea Island Company. Coffin's young apprentice, friend and cousin Alfred William Jones, was supervising his interests on Sapelo Island when Coffin called on him to manage Sea Island Company. Young Jones was indeed faced with a huge challenge because at that time there were no resorts between Pinehurst to the north and Daytona to the south, and many were skeptical that people of means would be attracted to a resort hotel on a remote Georgia island. There were other reasons to be concerned.

OVERCOMING OBSTACLES

The fulfillment of Coffin's vision for the island, which would ultimately lead to international acclaim, was faced with additional obstacles. There were no public utilities on the island, an electric plant had to be built, and a telephone system had to be installed. In addition, the remoteness of the island caused transportation problems for potential guests. Jones formed a transport company to shuttle guests to and from Savannah and Jacksonville, the nearest transportation hubs. With the opening of the Sea Island Golf Club and the remaking of a beach pavilion into the Casino, the Sea Island Company needed immediate accommodations for guests until the construction of a hotel could be finished. A multi-storied ship called the *Amphitrite* was obtained and docked at the company's boat landing on St. Simons. This floating hotel was equipped with every modern convenience including telephones and electric fans. By October of 1928, the hotel called The Cloister, designed by noted Palm Beach architect Addison Mizner, was in operation on Sea Island. At the same time it was being constructed, several other Sea Island Company projects were also underway and beginning to shape the area and Sea Island into a premier resort and residential destination.

AN END AND NEW BEGINNING

The impact of the Great Depression proved trying for the young Sea Island Company. With the stock market crash of 1929, Coffin was forced to sell his Sapelo Island assets to hold onto Sea Island. In the 1930s, Coffin spent much of his time trying to keep his empire together. His beloved wife died in 1932. Coffin himself died in 1937 and was buried next to Matilda in Christ Church Cemetery. Through the persistence and dedication of Alfred Jones, The Cloister became known as one of the finest resorts in America and one of the country's most distinguished and celebrated landmarks. Even in its earlier days, The Cloister's reputation as a sophisticated resort of international appeal drew authors, politicians, royalty, dignitaries and celebrities such as Eugene O'Neill, Somerset Maugham, Lillian Gish, John D. Rockefeller Jr., William Boyd (Hopalong Cassidy), and Jimmy Stewart, and U.S. Presidents Coolidge, Hoover, Eisenhower, Ford, and Carter, as well as George H.W. Bush, who had honeymooned at The Cloister in 1945. In June 2004, Sea Island hosted the G8 Summit, the most significant annual gathering of the leaders of the eight most powerful countries in the free world—Canada, France, Germany, Italy, Japan, Russia, the United Kingdom, and the United States, as well as the European Union— to discuss current world issues in a relaxed and open manner. In keeping with Sea Island's long-standing tradition begun by Calvin Coolidge in 1928, President George W. Bush and British Prime Minister Tony Blair planted live oaks on the grounds of The Cloister during the Summit.

SEA ISLAND TODAY

In addition to its unique oceanside setting, service, and amenities, Sea Island's renown as a world class destination is rooted in its devotion to the game of golf, with legendary names having designed and played its courses since Sea Island Golf Club opened in 1927. Today, Sea Island Resorts features two of the world's most exceptional destinations: The Cloister, on Sea Island, and The Lodge at Sea Island Golf Club, which opened in 2001. In 2003, after seventy-five years of service, Sea Island Company closed the original main building of The Cloister and replaced it with a new one even more distinctive than the first and yet highly reminiscent of the original. The Cloister remains an icon and inspires generations of guests to return again and again. In addition to The Cloister and The Lodge, the resort includes the Sea Island Beach Club, Golf Learning Center, three championship golf courses, a variety of dining options, outstanding children's programs and facilities, tennis courts, yacht club, shooting school, spa, and fitness center. Beyond the resort, the residential community of the island consists of large gracious homes with carefully manicured lawns and gardens. Arguably, the secluded retreat of Sea Island is the gem of Georgia's coastline.

CLOISTER BRUNSWICK STEW

1 tablespoon butter	1 cup cooked corn
1 medium onion, diced	1 cup cooked peas
1 garlic clove, diced	1 cup lima beans
16 ounces chicken broth	1 cup Cattleman BBQ Sauce
1 medium potato, medium dice	1 tablespoon tomato paste
1 pound smoked pork butt, shredded	1 tablespoon brown sugar
1 ounce medium diced tomatoes	1 tablespoon red hot pepper sauce
1 cup tomato juice	Salt and pepper to taste

Assemble ingredients and utensils. In a large stewing pot, over a low medium heat, melt butter, and sauté the onions and garlic, stirring frequently until the onions are translucent. Add the chicken broth, potatoes, tomato paste, diced tomatoes, tomato juice, and smoked pork. Bring the broth to a boil and stir occasionally. When the potatoes are done, add the BBQ sauce, brown sugar, hot sauce, corn, peas, and lima beans. Once it comes back to boiling, reduce heat to low and cover, then let simmer for at least 45 minutes stirring occasionally. Adjust seasoning.

Yields 4 large servings

Courtesy of The Cloister at Sea Island

KING AND PRINCE MUFFINS

2	cups all-purpose flour	3/4	cups chopped pecans
2	cups brown sugar	1/2	cup raisins
1/2	tablespoon baking soda	2	cups buttermilk
1/2	tablespoon salt	2	sticks butter, melted
1	tablespoon baking powder	2	eggs
1/4	cups oatmeal		

Assemble all ingredients and utensils. Preheat oven to 350 degrees. Combine the flour, brown sugar, baking soda, salt, baking powder, and oatmeal. Add the buttermilk, eggs, and melted butter. Mix for 30 seconds. Scrape down the bowl. Add pecans and raisins and mix at low speed for about 15 seconds, or until ingredients are moistened. Fill lightly greased muffin tins 1/2 full. Bake in oven for 25 minutes. Let stand 5 minutes.

Yields 2 dozen

Courtesy of the Chef's Collection at King and Prince Resort

SPINACH SUPREME

    2   10-ounce packages frozen chopped spinach
    3   slices bacon, cooked and crumbled
    1   6-ounce can sliced mushrooms, drained
  1/4   teaspoon marjoram
    1   8-ounce carton sour cream
    1   cup grated sharp cheddar cheese

Assemble all ingredients and utensils. Preheat oven to 325 degrees. Cook spinach by package directions. Combine all ingredients except cheese. Put into greased 1 1/2 quart casserole. Bake for 20–25 minutes. Sprinkle with cheese and return to oven for 5 minutes

Yields 8 servings

TWICE-BAKED NEW POTATOES

   12   small new potatoes
  1/4   cup butter
  1/2   cup grated Cheddar cheese
  1/4   cup milk
    1   teaspoon dried basil
    1   teaspoon paprika
  1/2   teaspoon garlic salt
  1/2   teaspoon pepper
  1/4   cup instant potato flakes
    2   tablespoons freshly grated Parmesan cheese
        Paprika

Assemble ingredients and utensils. Preheat the oven to 400 degrees. Bake potatoes with skins on a baking sheet for 20 minutes. Let sit until cool enough to handle. Cut each potato in half and use a melon baller to gently scoop potatoes out to form tiny "bowls" about 1/4-inch thick. In a medium bowl, combine the potato pulp and remaining ingredients and use a fork to combine well. Carefully refill each skin with the mixture; they should overflow a little. Sprinkle paprika over top and bake for 10 to 15 minutes, until heated through.

Yields 8 servings

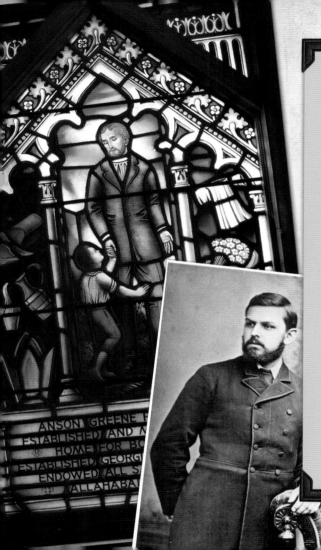

A DESTINATION OF INSPIRATION

Christ Church, nestled among the towering oaks of a quaint, peaceful cemetery, was built in 1820 and is one of the oldest churches in Georgia. As one of St. Simons Island's most treasured landmarks, it was here that John and Charles Wesley, two brothers from England who are considered the founders of Methodism, first preached to the settlers of Ft. Frederica beneath the limbs of a huge gnarled oak tree that still stands. The building was partially destroyed by occupying Union troops during the Civil War and was rebuilt in 1884 by Anson Phelps Dodge Jr. in memory of his wife, Ellen. Today, it is the trusted keeper of treasures within and without. Its rustic interior is highlighted by magnificent stained glass windows commemorating the early history of the church and St. Simons Island including the founding of Georgia by General James Oglethorpe, and the ministry of John and Charles Wesley at Frederica. Still another window with a biblical scene has been authenticated as an unsigned Tiffany masterpiece. Its beautiful, alluring cemetery contains the grave of beloved author Eugenia Price and those of many of the people upon whom she based her books as well as many historic figures of the area. It beckons visitors from around the world who find it the perfect spot for reflection.

COCONUT BREAD

1	egg	3	teaspoons baking powder
1 1/2	cups milk	1/2	teaspoon salt
1/2	teaspoon vanilla extract	1/4	teaspoon ground cinnamon
1/4	teaspoon coconut extract	1	cup sugar
1	cup flaked coconut		
3	cups all-purpose flour		

Assemble ingredients and utensils. Preheat the oven to 350 degrees. Combine egg, milk, extracts, and coconut in a blender container. Blend for 30 seconds. Sift the dry ingredients together in a bowl. Pour the liquid mixture over the dry ingredients. Stir to combine; do not beat. Pour the batter into a greased 9x5-inch loaf pan. Bake for one hour and 10 minutes. Let cool completely. Remove from pan, wrap, and refrigerate. Serve chilled.

Yields 1 loaf of 8 servings

KING AND PRINCE LOW COUNTRY SHRIMP AND GRITS

2	ounces water	8	beef bouillon cubes
1	pound 26–30 shrimp	1	quart water
3/4	cup sliced mushrooms	4	ounces Burgundy wine
1/2	cup julienned red pepper	4	ounces of 1/2 cornstarch
1/2	cup julienned green		and 1/2 water, mixed
	pepper		Dash of salt
1/2	cup julienned onion		Dash of cayenne pepper

Assemble ingredients and utensils. Sauté onions, mushrooms, and peppers in butter. Add wine and bring to a boil. Add salt and cayenne pepper, reduce heat. Add shrimp and simmer for 5 minutes. Add beef bouillon cubes and mix well, add water, and bring to boil. Thicken with cornstarch/water mixture.

Place portion cooked grits into bowl. Ladle portion of shrimp and gravy over grits. Garnish with parmesan or parsley.

CHEESE GRITS

2	cups stone ground grits	1 1/2	cups Monterey Jack
1	quart chicken stock		cheese
1	quart milk	1/4	cup water

Assemble ingredients and utensils. Bring chicken stock and milk to boil. Add grits, cook for 5 minutes. Add cheese, reduce heat, and simmer for 5 minutes. Add butter, stir well, and cook for 10 minutes.

Courtesy of the Chef's Collection at King and Prince Resort

St. Simons
World-Renowned Storyteller

Eugenia Price, already a noted author of inspirational nonfiction, fell in love with St. Simons while on a promotional book tour in Florida in 1961. A serendipitous side trip to the island sealed her destiny. The graves at Christ Church's cemetery captured her imagination and "The rest," they say, "is history." In 1965, she and companion Joyce Blackburn moved from Chicago to St. Simons, and Eugenia's career as one of the United States' greatest writers of detailed historical fiction was born. She blended biography, history, and masterful storytelling set in the American South into critically acclaimed works, such as the St Simons Trilogy which were based on real people. Her meticulously researched books set the standard for historical fiction of the period and helped create the Christian romance genre. In addition, Eugenia's Florida Trilogy, Savannah Quartet, Georgia Trilogy, and twenty-five other works of fiction and nonfiction became popular in sixteen foreign countries. Because many of her millions of readers quickly fall in love with her settings and her accounting of Island families, they come from around the world to visit the island and the cemetery in which Eugenia Price was laid to rest in 1996 near many of the characters who had originally provided her inspiration.

EUGENIA PRICE
JUNE 22, 1916
MAY 28, 1996

U. S. COAST GUARD STATION, EAST BEACH, ST. SIMONS ISLAND, NEAR BRUNSWICK, GA.—27

MACADAMIA CRUSTED MAHI

4	8-ounce portions of Mahi-Mahi	2	cups Japanese bread crumbs
2	cups egg wash (3 eggs mixed with 1 cup milk)	1	cup macadamia nuts
1	cup all-purpose flour	4	tablespoons olive oil
			Salt and pepper

Assemble all ingredients and utensils. Preheat oven to 350 degrees. Blend together bread crumbs and macadamia nuts in food processor. Set aside. Preheat olive oil in sauté pan. Season Mahi-Mahi with salt and pepper on each side. Dredge in flour lightly and then place in egg wash, thoroughly coating each filet, and place in breadcrumb/nut mixture, coating evenly. Place each filet in olive oil browning on each side. Place in oven on baking sheet for 8 to 10 minutes. Time may vary based on thickness of Mahi filets.

Yields 4 servings

TOMATOES WITH SPINACH SOUFFLÉ

8   small to medium tomatoes
2   tablespoons prepared
    mustard
8   slices bacon, diced and
    sautéed
1   10-ounce package frozen
    spinach, thawed and drained

2   eggs, beaten
2   tablespoons milk
1   teaspoon garlic salt
1   teaspoon pepper
1/4 cup grated Parmesan cheese
    Parsley sprigs for garnish

Assemble ingredients and utensils. Cut a thin slice from the top of each tomato. Scoop out pulp to make a shell. Drain the shell upside down for 15 minutes. Preheat the oven to 375 degrees. Spread mustard inside of each tomato shell. Divide bacon evenly between tomatoes. In a blender, mix spinach, eggs, milk, and seasonings. Spoon the spinach mixture into the tomatoes. Sprinkle 1 teaspoon cheese over the top of each. Bake, uncovered, for 15 to 20 minutes, or until golden brown on top. Garnish with parsley sprigs.

Yields 8 servings

POLYNESIAN PORK SATAY

12   ounces lean pork, cubed
4   wooden skewers
1   lime, halved
2   cloves garlic, crushed
1   cup coconut milk
1/4   cup brown sugar
1   tablespoon orange juice
3   tablespoons teriyaki sauce
3   tablespoons sesame seeds

Assemble ingredients and utensils. Divide pork into 4 three-ounce portions, skewer, and place in a shallow baking dish. Squeeze half of the lime over pork. Spread garlic over pork. Pour coconut milk over top. Cover and refrigerate for 1 hour, turning occasionally. Preheat the broiler. In a small bowl, combine brown sugar, orange juice, and teriyaki sauce, along with juice from the remaining lime half. Stir well. Lift pork from the marinade and place on a broiling rack. Use a pastry brush to baste pork with the brown sugar sauce. Broil, basting and turning frequently for 8 to 10 minutes. Sprinkle pork with sesame seeds just before serving.

Yields 4 servings

BIBB LETTUCE WITH CAPER AND EGG DRESSING

1   hard-boiled egg
1/4   cup red or white wine vinegar
1/2   teaspoon chopped chives
3/4   cup oil (1/2 olive, 1/4 corn)
1   tablespoon capers
1/4   teaspoon dry mustard
1   tablespoon lemon juice
1/4   teaspoon salt
6–8   heads Bibb lettuce
      Cracked pepper

Assemble ingredients and utensils. Chop egg finely. Combine all ingredients, except lettuce, in a jar and shake well. Wash and tear lettuce. Dry thoroughly and crisp in the refrigerator. Pour dressing over lettuce just before serving. Can refrigerate dressing for months.

Yields 8 to 10 servings

CLOISTER FRIED LOBSTER TAIL

4	4–6 ounce Maine lobster tails	1	tablespoon salt
2	cups flour	1	tablespoon pepper
2	cups buttermilk		Heavy bottom pot 1/2 full of frying oil (approx 1 1/2 quarts)
1/4	cup Old Bay Seasoning		

Assemble ingredients and utensils. Clean the lobster tails, devein, and make sure that it is free from any shell. Mix flour, Old Bay Seasoning, salt, and pepper in a bowl. Heat the oil in the pot up to 350 degrees. Dredge the lobster in the flour mix, shake off excess flour, then dip in the buttermilk. Let the excess drip off and then dredge back through the flour. Place in the hot oil, and cook for 4 to 5 minutes pending size of the lobster. When ready, remove with a slotted spoon carefully draining the excess oil, place on absorbent paper for a minute or two to rest. Serve with a honey mustard or Remoulaude sauce.

Yields 4 servings

Courtesy of The Cloister at Sea Island

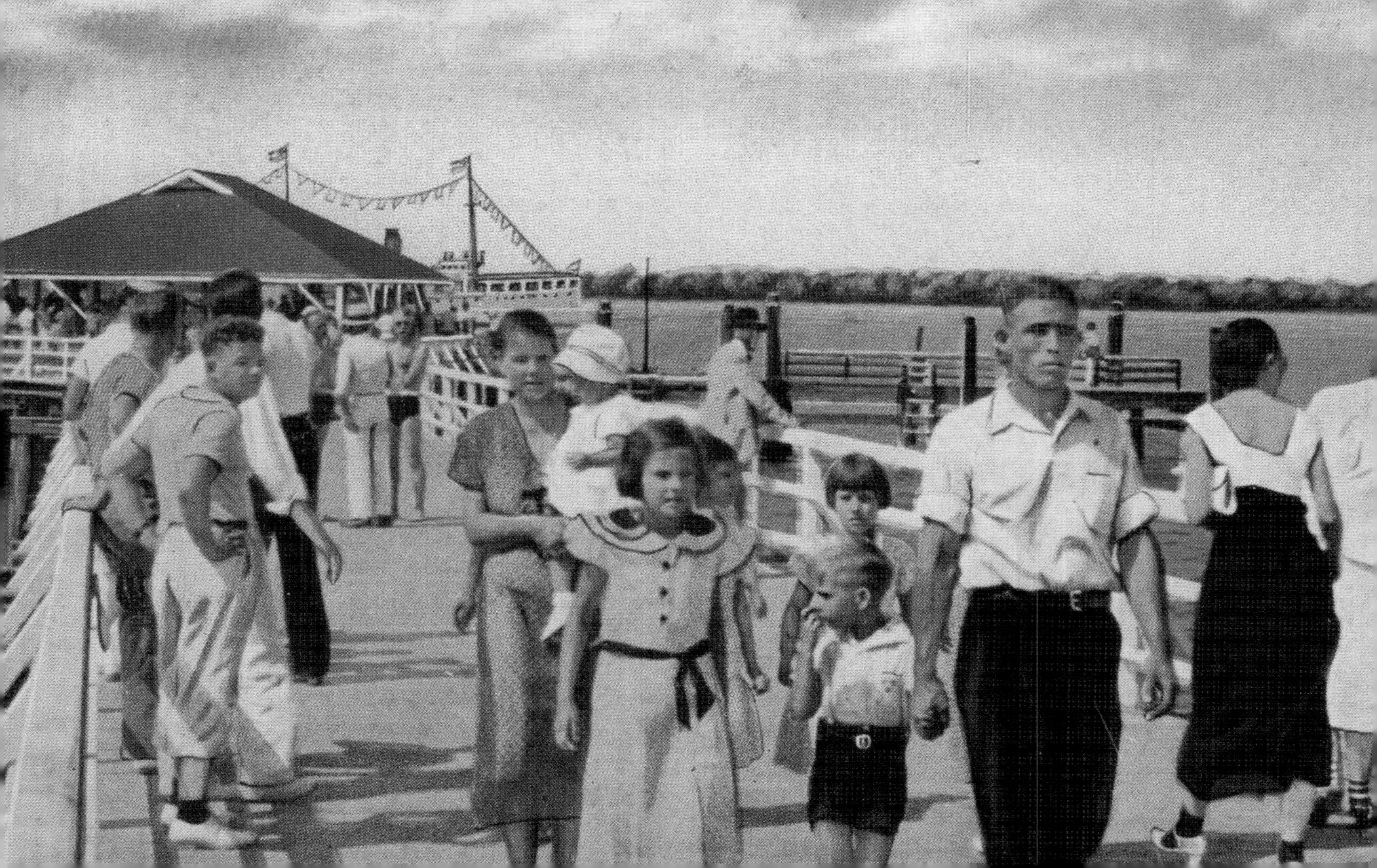

ST. SIMONS PIER, ST. SIMONS, GEORGIA (NEAR BRUNSWICK)—20

BEST ORANGE SALAD

1   3-ounce package orange gelatin
1   3-ounce package lemon gelatin
2   cups boiling water
1 1/2   cups cold water

1   cup drained, crushed pineapple
2   large bananas, mashed
1 1/2   cups miniature marshmallows

Assemble ingredients and untensils. Combine gelatins with boiling water; add cold water. Place in refrigerator. When mixture begins to set, add remaining ingredients. Refrigerate until set.

TOPPING

2/3   cup sugar
3   tablespoons all purpose flour
    Pinch of salt
2   tablespoons butter, melted

1   egg, beaten
1   cup pineapple juice
1   8-ounce container non-dairy whipped topping

Mix first 4 topping ingredients. Add egg; add juice, mixing well. Cook until thick. Cool; fold in whipped topping and mix. Spread on orange salad.

Yields 6 to 9 servings

BUTTERMILK POTATO SALAD

1	small onion, chopped	1	tablespoon white vinegar
3/4	cup mayonnaise	1	teaspoon garlic salt
1/4	cup sour cream	2	ribs celery, chopped
1/4	cup buttermilk	6	medium potatoes, peeled,
1	tablespoon Dijon mustard		boiled until firm-tender,
1	teaspoon pepper		and cubed

Assemble ingredients and utensils. Mix onion, mayonnaise, sour cream, buttermilk, mustard, pepper, vinegar, and garlic salt in a large resealable container. Add celery and potatoes and toss gently. Chill overnight.

Yields 10 to 12 servings

Greetings from **SAINT SIMONS ISLAND GEORGIA**

KING AND PRINCE FLORIDA CREOLE BLACK GROUPER

1 pound black grouper (four 8-ounce portions)	1 2-pound bag fresh spinach
3 tablespoons olive oil	2 ounces clarified butter
2–3 tablespoons blackening seasoning	Creole Sauce (See recipe below)

Preheat grill. Dip each grouper portion in olive oil, sprinkle blackening seasoning over each side. Place on grill, cook for 5 minutes on each side until fish is translucent and flaky. Sauté spinach in butter, set to the side. Place spinach on plate and grouper filet on top of spinach. Ladle sauce over fish. Garnish with chopped green onion and paprika.

CREOLE SAUCE

1 tablespoon olive oil	4 ounces white wine
4 ounces medium size shrimp, peeled and deveined	1 tablespoon Creole or Cajun seasoning
4 ounces lump crab meat	1/2 teaspoon cayenne pepper
1 stalk green onion, finely chopped	2 cups heavy whipping cream

In sauce pot in hot oil, sauté shrimp, green onion, Creole/Cajun seasoning, and cayenne pepper until shrimp is almost cooked through. Deglaze with white wine and reduce by half. Add heavy whipping cream and bring to boil. Turn down to simmer and let reduce until smooth creamy consistency. Add crab meat, stirring lightly so as not to break up lumps.

Courtesy of the Chef's Collection at King and Prince Resort

ISLAND ICE CREAM BALLS

1 cup diced mango
  (or use dried if fresh is unavailable)
2 pints vanilla ice cream, softened
1/2 cup sweetened flaked coconut
1/2 cup crushed macadamia nuts

Assemble ingredients and utensils. Carefully fold mango into ice cream. Scoop 4 rounded balls of ice cream onto individual pieces of plastic wrap. Seal the plastic wrap tightly and freeze for at least 2 1/2 hours. Remove the plastic-wrapped ice cream balls from the freezer and let sit at room temperature for 5 to 10 minutes. Unwrap and roll in coconut and macadamia nuts. Serve immediately.

Yields 4 servings

MAPLE BRANDY MILKSHAKE

4 1/2 cups milk
  1/3 cup maple syrup
    6 shots brandy
    6 scoops vanilla ice cream

Assemble ingredients and utensils. Combine all ingredients in a blender container. Pulse until the mixture reaches milkshake consistency. Serve immediately.

Yields 6 servings

A "TUG OF WAR" AT EAST BEACH, ST. SIMONS ISLAND, GA.—24

VILLAGE CREEK CRABMEAT CASSEROLE

8	slices white bread	4	eggs, beaten
2	pounds select crabmeat	1	teaspoon salt
3/4	cup mayonnaise		White pepper to taste
1	medium onion, finely chopped	1	10 3/4-ounce can mushroom soup
1	medium green pepper, finely chopped	1	cup grated American cheese
1	cup celery, finely chopped		Paprika to taste
3	cups milk		

Assemble ingredients and utensils. Grease a 13-inch casserole and put in half the bread diced. Mix the crabmeat, mayonnaise, onion, green pepper, and celery, and place on diced bread in casserole. Trim crust from the remaining bread and place in slices on top of crabmeat mixture. Mix beaten eggs, milk, salt, and pepper and pour over all. Let stand overnight in refrigerator.

Next day pour on undiluted soup but Do Not Mix. Sprinkle with cheese and paprika. Bake for 1 hour in 325-degree oven.

Yields 8 servings

SEA ISLAND SPICY SHRIMP

    2   pounds or 20–25 shrimp, peeled and deveined
    1   tablespoon chopped shallots
    1   teaspoon chopped garlic
  1/4   cup vegetable oil
  1/4   cup white wine
    1   lemon, juiced
    1   tablespoon Sambal
    1   tablespoon Old Bay Seasoning
        Salt and pepper to taste
    1   cup vegetable oil

Assemble ingredients and utensils. Mix shrimp, shallots, garlic, Old Bay Seasoning, and 1/4 cup oil and marinate for 1 hour. Heat up a heavy bottom pan and add 1 cup oil, heat up and add the shrimp just before the oil starts to smoke. Using a spoon, stir the shrimp making sure that they start to cook evenly. Half way through the process add wine, lemon juice, and Sambal. Mix thoroughly. As soon as the wine is added the cooking process will speed up, and the shrimp should be ready in about 5 minutes. Adjust seasoning as required.

Yields 4 servings

Recipes Courtesy of The Cloister at Sea Island

ALMOND RICE

    1   cup butter, melted
    2   cups raw long-grain white rice
    1   cup slivered almonds
    2   tablespoons chopped green bell pepper
    2   tablespoons chopped green onion
    1   pound mushrooms, sliced
    6   cups chicken broth

Assemble ingredients and utensils. Preheat oven to 350 degrees. In a large heavy skillet or saucepan, combine all ingredients, except chicken broth. Cook until rice turns yellow, stirring constantly. Combine the mixture with chicken broth. Pour into 1 large or 2 medium buttered casserole dishes. Cover tightly and bake for 1 hour, or until firm.

Yields 18 to 20 servings

EGGPLANT CASSEROLE

1	medium onion, chopped	3	eggs, beaten
1	tablespoon butter	1 1/2	cups mild Cheddar cheese, shredded
2	cups eggplant, cooked, drained and mashed	1	cup cornbread, crumbled or 1 cup cracker crumbs
1	16-ounce can tomatoes, drained and mashed		Salt and pepper to taste

Assemble ingredients and utensils. Preheat oven to 350 degrees. Sauté onion in butter until golden; add eggplant and tomatoes, mix well. Stir eggs into warm mixture, stirring until thick, like scrambled eggs. Add cheese and 3/4 cup of crumbs, salt and pepper. Turn into buttered casserole. Add remaining crumbs. Bake for 30 minutes.

Yields 6 servings

KING AND PRINCE CRABCAKES

1/2 pound super lump crab meat	1 egg
1/2 pound claw meat	1 ounce mayonnaise
2 tablespoons diced red bell pepper	1 tablespoon blackening spice
2 tablespoons diced green bell pepper	1 tablespoon Habanero sauce
Olive oil	1/2 cup Japanese bread crumbs
	1/2 teaspoon kosher salt

Assemble ingredients and utensils. Preheat oven to 400 degrees. Sauté peppers in olive oil until tender, set to side to cool. Keep sauté pan ready. Place lump crabmeat and claw meat in bowl, mix together. Do not break up lumps. Mix egg, mayonnaise, blackening spice, and Habanero sauce together. Fold gently into crab mixture until well incorporated. Add peppers and bread crumbs, fold in. Season with salt.

Using a pastry cutter circle, form 4 cakes. Brown each cake in sauté pan. Place on baking sheet and bake in oven for 5 to 8 minutes.

Yields 4 servings

Courtesy of the Chef's Collection at King and Prince Resort

The King and Prince Hotel, St. Simons Island, Ga.

MINT TEA

4 individual tea bags	6 cups cold water
14 large mint leaves	
3 cups boiling water	Garnish:
1 cup sugar	8 sprigs mint
1/4 cup fresh lemon juice	1 orange, sliced
1 cup orange juice	1 lemon, sliced

Assemble all ingredients and utensils. Place tea bags and mint leaves in a large pitcher. Add boiling water and allow to steep for 10 minutes. Add sugar and stir very gently. Cool completely; stir and strain mixture. Discard tea bags and mint. Pour mixture back in pitcher; add remaining ingredients. Serve over ice in tea glasses. Garnish with mint and slices of fruit.

Yields 8 to 10 servings

CLOISTER PECAN PIE FILLING

7	ounces granulated sugar	15	ounces light corn syrup
3	ounces butter, melted	4	whole eggs
14	ounces pecan halves		Pinch of salt

Assemble ingredients and utensils. Fill the raw pie shell half way with pecan halves. Mix the rest of the ingredients together thoroughly, and pour over the pecans to the top of the pie. Bake in 300-degree oven.

PECAN PIE SHELL

6	ounces butter	2	egg yolks
8	ounces cake flour		Pinch of Salt
2	ounces milk		

Assemble ingredients and utensils. Mix butter and flour together until pea size pieces are achieved. Add milk, yolks, and salt. Mix into a smooth dough and refrigerate for an hour. Roll the dough on a flat surface into a circle, and fit onto a pie pan.

Yields 1 9-inch shell

Courtesy of The Cloister at Sea Island

A GUIDING LIGHT

The picturesque lighthouse at St. Simons Island is the oldest brick structure in the area and one of the most beautiful lighthouses in the South. The original structure was the longtime dream of a young architect named James Gould whose desire to build a lighthouse began when he was a young boy. In 1807 that dream came true, and he was actually hired as the chief architect in its construction. In 1810, President Madison appointed him as the lighthouse's first keeper where he remained for twenty-seven years. In 1862, the lighthouse was destroyed by the Confederate Army to prevent it from being an aid to the navigation of U.S. warships. The current lighthouse, built by Charles Cluskey who was one of Georgia's most renowned architects, was completed in 1872. Unfortunately, he died of malaria a year before it was completed. It is a 104-foot structure with a cast iron spiral stairway consisting of 129 steps leading to the top. In 1953, the oil lamps and chains that originally lit the first lighthouse were replaced by a biconvex Fresnel lens (French for hand-made) and timers that eliminated the need for a lighthouse keeper. The keeper's residence has been turned into a museum, and the lighthouse is still maintained as an operational light by the U.S. Coast Guard.

FRIED FISH WITH HOMEMADE TARTAR SAUCE

20–30 6-ounce fish fillets
Salt and pepper to taste
1 cup prepared mustard
1 teaspoon Tabasco sauce

2 tablespoons Worcestershire sauce
3 cups yellow cornmeal
4 quarts oil, or amount
needed to fill a 12-quart, heavy iron pot

Assemble ingredients and utensils. Salt and pepper fillets. Combine mustard with Tabasco and Worcestershire; coat fillets with mixture and allow to set for about 30 minutes. Put cornmeal in a bag and shake coated fillets in meal. Heat oil in a heavy iron pot to about 380 degrees. Fry fish, one layer deep, in hot oil for 2 1/2 minutes, or until they rise to the top. Drain on paper towels.

Yields 10 servings

HOMEMADE TARTAR SAUCE

1 cup mayonnaise
1/3 cup dill pickle relish
1 teaspoon lemon juice
1 tablespoon onion, finely
minced

1 teaspoon garlic salt
1 tablespoon fresh parsley,
minced

Assemble ingredients and utensils. Thoroughly mix all ingredients. Cover and refrigerate overnight.

Yields about 1 1/2 cups sauce

BAKED SEAFOOD SALAD

1   small green pepper, chopped
1   small onion, chopped
1   cup celery, chopped
1   pound crab meat
1   pound raw shrimp, peeled and deveined
1   cup mayonnaise

1/2   teaspoon salt
1   teaspoon Worcestershire sauce
1   cup buttered bread crumbs
    Pepper to taste
    Seafood seasoning

Assemble ingredients and utensils. Preheat oven to 350 degrees. Cook and clean shrimp. Mix all ingredients except bread crumbs and put in casserole. Sprinkle buttered bread crumbs on top. Grated cheese may also be added to crumb topping. Bake for 30 minutes.

Yields 6 servings

An Island Treasure

St. Simons' oldest standing church was built in 1880 by Norman Dodge and originally named St. James Union Church. It was repaired in 1897 after a hurricane. In 1911, because it was no longer used for services, it was de-consecrated, moved to its present location, and used as a recreational center. In 1948, the Methodist Church purchased 43.5 acres of what had been the beautiful Hamilton Plantation along the banks of the Frederica River, and thus, Epworth-by-the-Sea was born. The new retreat center was named for the small town of Epworth, England where John and Charles Wesley were born. The chapel, renamed Lovely Lane (in honor of the Baltimore, Maryland site where, in 1784, just after the American Revolution, the historic founding conference of American Methodism was held and Francis Asbury ordained the first Methodist Bishop in America), was re-consecrated and restored under the leadership of Bishop Arthur J. Moore in 1950. The magnificent stained glass windows are irreplaceable pieces of Old English Art Glass. The retreat center flourished under the leadership of Bishop Moore. Epworth-by-the-Sea, operated by the South Georgia Conference of the United Methodist Church, is now a Christian conference and retreat Center where more than a hundred thousand visitors of all faiths convene annually.

CLOISTER CORN MUFFINS

1	cup butter	1 1/4	cups bread flour
1/2	cup sugar	1 1/2	cups cornmeal
3	whole eggs	3	tablespoons baking powder
1/4	cup bacon bits	1 1/2	teaspoons salt
2	cups creamed corn	2	tablespoons milk
1	cup grated Cheddar cheese		

Assemble ingredients and utensils. Combine butter and sugar in a mixing bowl, cream until it is very soft. Add eggs slowly until incorporated. Add remaining ingredients, mix on a slow speed until everything looks like a soft batter. Chill batter for up to 5 hours. Scoop into well greased muffin pans. Bake in a 450-degree oven for 15 to 20 minutes. Make sure that surface is golden brown. Completely cool muffins and then release from pan.

Yields 24 medium muffins

Courtesy of The Cloister at Sea Island

RUM PUDDING WITH RASPBERRY SAUCE

1	3-ounce package unflavored gelatin	1	cup sugar
1/2	cup cold water	1	cup light rum
3	cups boiling water	3	cups heavy cream, whipped
6	egg yolks		

Assemble ingredients and utensils. Soften gelatin in cold water in a bowl. Dissolve this mixture in boiling water. Cool in the refrigerator, stirring occasionally, until the mixture becomes thickened. Beat egg yolks with sugar until lemon colored. Gradually stir into the cooled and slightly thickened gelatin mixture. Stir in rum. Whip cream and fold into mixture. Spray 16 one-half cup molds with nonstick cooking spray for easy removal. Pour the mixture into molds and chill. Top with Raspberry Sauce when ready to serve.

Yields 16 to 20 servings

RASPBERRY SAUCE

4	10-ounce packages frozen raspberries
2	cups sugar

In a large saucepan, combine raspberries and sugar. Boil for 5 minutes, pressing the berries to release juices. Strain and chill. Serve over Rum Pudding.

Yields about 4 cups sauce

PARTY GUACAMOLE

```
2    cloves garlic
4    medium soft avocados
1    teaspoon lemon juice
4    green onions, chopped
4    medium tomatoes, chopped
2    tablespoons chopped green bell pepper
1/4  teaspoon Tabasco sauce
     Salt to taste
     Mayonnaise to thicken (if needed)
     Boston or baby lettuce for serving
     Tortilla chips
```

Assemble ingredients and utensils. In a large bowl, mash garlic and scrape it out of the bowl. Mash avocados in the same bowl and add lemon juice. Mix in remaining ingredients. Serve on beds of lettuce or in your favorite serving dish with tortilla chips.

Yields 12 to 16 servings

ORANGE JULIUS

```
1    6-ounce frozen orange juice
1    cup milk
1    cup water
1/2  cup sugar
1    teaspoon vanilla
12   ice cubes
```

Assemble ingredients and utensils. Combine all ingredients in blender. Cover and blend until smooth, about 30 seconds.

Yields 3 to 4 servings

VEGETABLE KABOBS

    2   tablespoons soy sauce
    1   teaspoon spicy mustard
    1   tablespoon water
   24   mushrooms, cleaned
    2   purple onions, cut into 1 1/2-inch chunks
    1   red bell pepper, cut into 1 1/2-inch pieces
        Wooden skewers

Assemble ingredients and utensils. Combine soy sauce, mustard, and water in a small bowl. Skewer vegetables and place on the grill. Use a pastry brush to baste with the sauce during grilling.

Yields 6 servings

COUNTRY COLESLAW

  1/2   head cabbage, shredded
    1   onion, shredded
    2   carrots, shredded
    1   teaspoon sugar
  1/4   cup mayonnaise
    1   tablespoon apple cider vinegar
        Salt and pepper to taste

Assemble ingredients and utensils. In a large bowl, combine all ingredients. Mix well and chill for several hours before serving.

Yields 8 servings

KING AND PRINCE WILD GEORGIA SHRIMP AND CRAB LASAGNA

1 package precooked lasagna sheets	1 pound lumb crab meat
4 cups Mornay sauce (see recipe below)	1 medium onion, diced
1 pound medium shrimp (preferably Wild Georgia Shrimp)	1 green onion, diced
	2 cups mozzarella cheese, shredded
	4 ounces butter
	Salt and pepper

Preheat oven to 350 degrees. Pull and thaw 4 precooked lasagna sheets. Set aside. Saute onion and green onion in butter until translucent. Season with salt and pepper. Add shrimp and cook until done. Add crabmeat, toss together. Set aside. Grease 9x11 baking pan, place one sheet of lasagna on bottom. Spread Mornay sauce over sheet with spatula. Sprinkle shrimp and crab mixture over Mornay. Sprinkle mozzarella cheese over shrimp and crab mixture. Continue layering in order. Spread Mornay over top sheet and sprinkle with last of cheese.

MORNAY SAUCE

4 cups heavy cream, warmed to room temperature	8 tablespoons flour
8 tablespoons butter	1 cup mozzarella cheese, shredded
	Salt and pepper to taste

Over medium heat, melt butter in a sauce pan. Add flour, whisking until smooth. Add warm cream and continue to whisk until thick and bubbly. Remove from heat and add cheese. Season to taste.

Courtesy of the Chef's Collection at King and Prince Resort

HERB CRUSTED PORK

1	5- to 6-pound pork loin roast
1	tablespoon garlic salt
1	tablespoon black pepper
1/2	tablespoon rubbed sage
2	tablespoons Worcestershire sauce
1/2	tablespoon paprika
2	tablespoons dried basil

1	tablespoon dried oregano
1	tablespoon crushed dried rosemary leaves
1/2	tablespoon red pepper flakes, optional
1/2	lemon

Assemble ingredients and utensils. Preheat the oven to 325 degrees. Carefully rinse pork and pat dry with paper towels. Briskly rub garlic salt all over tenderloin, working it in thoroughly. Repeat, one at a time, with remaining ingredients. Place tenderloin in a baking dish and squeeze lemon over the top. Cover with aluminum foil and bake for 2 1/2 to 3 1/2 hours, or until the internal temperature reaches 170 degrees. Remove the foil for the last 10 to 15 minutes before slicing.

Yields 10 to 12 servings

PECAN PUFFS

1/2 cup butter, melted
1 cup all-purpose flour
2 tablespoons sugar
1 teaspoon vanilla extract
1 cup chopped pecans
Confectioners' sugar

Assemble ingredients and utensils. Preheat the oven to 350 degrees. In a bowl, combine all ingredients, except confectioners' sugar, and shape into quarter-size balls. Bake for 20 to 25 minutes. Remove from the oven, cool slightly, and roll in sifted confectioners' sugar.

Yields 24 puffs

WARM BANANA MOUSSE

3 eggs
1 cup sugar
1/2 cup half-and-half, warmed to room temperature
1 teaspoon vanilla extract
3 ripe bananas, mashed
1 1/2 cups whipping cream, stiffly beaten
Vanilla wafers

Assemble ingredients and utensils. In the top of a double boiler over hot water (not boiling), beat eggs and sugar until frothy and pale yellow. Beat in light cream and vanilla. Beat in bananas. Allow the mixture to cool slightly and serve with whipped cream and vanilla wafers.

Yields 8 to 12 servings

To order additional copies of

MEET ME ON ST. SIMONS ISLAND

please e-mail
customerservice@SWPublishingGroup.com
or call 800-358-0560

DESCRIPTIONS OF PHOTOGRAPHS

Unless otherwise noted, photographic images are provided courtesy of the St. Simons Island Collection. Photographs provided by The Cloister at Sea Island are indicated by TCSI at the end of the photo description. The many images contributed by Mary Lawson Photography are identified as MLP. In addition, her supplemental artistic images appear on pages 59, 70, 78, 109. Vintage photographs are courtesy of the Coastal Georgia Historical Society.

RECIPE INDEX